Name

Copyright and Legal

Copyright

All rights reserved. No part of this planner may be reproduced in any form without expressed permission from the publisher, except in the case of brief quotations.

Legal and Disclaimer

This planner should not be considered a legally binding document. It is recommended you consult with a lawyer to create a formal, legally binding will regarding your desired final wishes and arrangements should you become incapacitated, or upon passing.

The author, publisher, and all those involved in the creation of this workbook, under any and all circumstances, are not considered responsible or liable for any damages that come from its content or purchase. Use of this planner is meant entirely for the benefit of the purchaser in the organization and documentation for end of life wishes and preferences.

It is a good idea to ensure those involved in your end of life planning and arrangements are notified of this document and its location. Important, sensitive and private content such as personal identification information and passwords are included in the following pages, and it is essential this information not become misplaced to avoid the risk of identity theft or misuse of any kind.

The owner and users of this document takes full responsibility for the safekeeping, accuracy, and content upon use. The user agrees this planner is considered an organizational workbook only, in which to record final wishes and desires relevant in the case of incapacitation or upon passing.

Table of Contents

Introduction

Welcome to your Peace of Mind and Heart Planner. This book is designed to make life-planning as simple, user friendly, and stress-free as possible.

Your Planner is a comprehensive, customizable, all-in-one workbook to record your vital information, personal wishes, and final messages to loved ones.

It is a valuable gift for those left behind so that they can ensure your instructions are fulfilled accordingly, and to help avoid duress or confusion by planning in advance.

We have provided plenty of space to customize each section as per your needs, and include additional overflow space at the back of the book if required. It is wise to begin with the initial personal identification section first, and then proceed to one chapter at a time, collecting all the documentation and information in advance for efficiency sake.

Remember to update this planner as changes to your circumstances arise, such as new employment, investments, insurance, or adjustments to your personal wishes.

Please remember, this planner is not considered a legal document and should not be considered a formal will.

***Always store this workbook somewhere safe, to prevent sensitive, private information from getting into the wrong hands**.

Personal Information

My Legal Name

Address

Mailbox or P.O. Box Number

Mailbox Location

Key Location

Primary Phone Numbers

Spouse's Name / Maiden Name

Children's Names

Grandchildren's Names

Additional Dependents Names

Pets Names

Notes

Siblings Names

Mother's Name / Maiden Name

Father's Name

Ex-Spouse's Name/s

Notes

At The Time of My Passing

Please Contact the Following People upon My Passing or Incapacity

Spouse / Partner

Name

Contact Information

Notes

Healthcare Power of Attorney Agent

Name

Contact Information

Notes

Executor

Name

Contact Information

Notes

Family and Close Friends

Name

Contact Information

Relationship

Name

Contact Information

Relationship

Name

Contact Information

Relationship

Name

Contact Information

Relationship

Name

Contact Information

Relationship

Name

Contact Information

Relationship

Name

Relationship

Contact Information

Name

Relationship

Contact Information

Name

Relationship

Contact Information

Name

Relationship

Contact Information

Name

Relationship

Contact Information

Name

Relationship

Contact Information

Name

Relationship

Contact Information

Name

Relationship

Contact Information

Name

Relationship

Contact Information

Name

Relationship

Contact Information

Name

Relationship

Contact Information

Name

Relationship

Contact Information

Please Contact the Following People Upon My Passing or Incapacity

Name

Relationship

Contact Information

Name

Relationship

Contact Information

Name

Relationship

Contact Information

Name

Relationship

Contact Information

Name

Relationship

Contact Information

Name

Relationship

Contact Information

Please Contact the Following People Upon My Passing or Incapacity

Name

Relationship

Contact Information

Name

Relationship

Contact Information

Name

Relationship

Contact Information

Name

Relationship

Contact Information

Name

Relationship

Contact Information

Name

Relationship

Contact Information

Name

Relationship

Contact Information

Name

Relationship

Contact Information

Name

Relationship

Contact Information

Name

Relationship

Contact Information

Name

Relationship

Contact Information

Name

Relationship

Contact Information

Name

Relationship

Contact Information

Name

Relationship

Contact Information

Name

Relationship

Contact Information

Name

Relationship

Contact Information

Name

Relationship

Contact Information

Name

Relationship

Contact Information

Name

Relationship

Contact Information

Name

Relationship

Contact Information

Name

Relationship

Contact Information

Name

Relationship

Contact Information

Name

Relationship

Contact Information

Name

Relationship

Contact Information

Place of Worship: *Church, Synagogue, Etc.*

Name #1

Contact Information

Name #2

Contact Information

Notes

Lawyer #1

Name

Contact Information

Notes

Lawyer #2

Name

Contact Information

Notes

Estate Planner

Name

Contact Information

Notes

Business Employer / Associate

Company and Agent Name

Contact Information

Business Employer / Associate

Company and Agent Name

Contact Information

Business Employer / Associate

Company and Agent Name

Contact Information

Financial Advisor

Company and Agent Name

Contact Information

Financial Advisor

Name

Contact Information

Accountant

Company and Agent Name

Contact Information

Health Care Provider – Medical

Company and Agent Name

Contact Information

Health Care Provider – Dental

Company and Agent Name

Contact Information

Health Care Provider – Vision

Company and Agent Name

Contact Information

Health Care Provider – Other

Company and Agent Name

Contact Information

Veterinarian

Company and Agent Name

Contact Information

Veterinarian

Company and Agent Name

Contact Information

Other

Name

Contact Information

Name

Contact Information

Name

Contact Information

Name

Contact Information

Name

Contact Information

Name

Contact Information

Name

Contact Information

Name

Contact Information

Contact Information - Notes

Funeral Arrangements

Funeral Arrangements Contact Person

Name ____________________

Relationship ____________________

Church, Synagogue, Other

Name of Priest, Rabbi, Other ____________________

Contact Information ____________________

Funeral Home

Address ____________________

Contact Information ____________________

Cemetery or Crematorium

Plot / Address ____________________

Contact Information ____________________

Funeral Insurance Policy

Company Name ____________________

Contact Information ____________________

Notes

Burial

Headstone Details

Cremation

Ashes to be spread

Obituary

Please Include the Following

Please Include the Following Personal Message to My Loved Ones

Funeral Arrangements - Notes

Asset Overview - What My Loved Ones Can Expect

Note: *Please see will for detailed instructions and division of assets.*

Personal Residence Address

PO Box Location and Address

Partner / Co-Owner Names

Contact Information

Legal Documentation Location and Instructions

Keys Location and Miscellaneous Instructions

Alarm and Security Information

Utilities Warranties and Documentation Location

Upkeep Information and Document Location (Gardener, Etc.)

Notes

Investment Property / Second Home Address

Type of Property (Residential / Commercial)

PO Box Location and Address

Partner / Co-Owner Names

Contact Information

Legal Documentation Location and Instructions

Keys Location and Miscellaneous Instructions

Alarm and Security Information

Utilities Warranties and Documentation Location

Upkeep Information and Document Location (Gardener, Etc.)

Notes

Vehicle List: *Car, Motorcycle, Recreation Vehicle, Snowmobile, Etc.*

Vehicle

Year/Make/Model

VIN – ID

Ownership Documentation Location

Lease / Load Information

Keys Location

Notes

Vehicle

Year/Make/Model

VIN – ID

Ownership Documentation Location

Lease / Load Information

Keys Location

Notes

Vehicle List:

Vehicle

Year/Make/Model

VIN – ID

Ownership Documentation Location

Lease / Load Information

Keys Location

Notes

Vehicle

Year/Make/Model

VIN – ID

Ownership Documentation Location

Lease / Load Information

Keys Location

Notes

Vehicle List:

Vehicle

Year/Make/Model

VIN – ID

Ownership Documentation Location

Lease / Load Information

Keys Location

Notes

Vehicle

Year/Make/Model

VIN – ID

Ownership Documentation Location

Lease / Load Information

Keys Location

Notes

Investments: Stocks, Mutual Funds, and Other

Type

Location

Account Number

Contact Person

Documentation Location

Notes

Type

Location

Account Number

Contact Person

Documentation Location

Notes

Type

Location

Account Number

Contact Person

Documentation Location

Notes

Investments: Stocks, Mutual Funds, and Other

Type

Location

Account Number

Contact Person

Documentation Location

Notes

Type

Location

Account Number

Contact Person

Documentation Location

Notes

Type

Location

Account Number

Contact Person

Documentation Location

Notes

Investments: Stocks, Mutual Funds, and Other

Type

Location

Account Number

Contact Person

Documentation Location

Notes

Type

Location

Account Number

Contact Person

Documentation Location

Notes

Type

Location

Account Number

Contact Person

Documentation Location

Notes

Investments: Stocks, Mutual Funds, and Other

Type

Location

Account Number

Contact Person

Documentation Location

Notes

Type

Location

Account Number

Contact Person

Documentation Location

Notes

Type

Location

Account Number

Contact Person

Documentation Location

Notes

Insurance Benefits

Policy Type

Location

Account Number

Contact Person

Documentation Location

Notes

Policy Type

Location

Account Number

Contact Person

Documentation Location

Notes

Policy Type

Location

Account Number

Contact Person

Documentation Location

Notes

Insurance Benefits

Policy Type

Location

Account Number

Contact Person

Documentation Location

Notes

Policy Type

Location

Account Number

Contact Person

Documentation Location

Notes

Policy Type

Location

Account Number

Contact Person

Documentation Location

Notes

Employer Benefits #1

Name

Account Number

Contact Person

Documentation Location

Notes

Employer Benefits #2

Name

Account Number

Contact Person

Documentation Location

Notes

Employer Benefits #3

Name

Account Number

Contact Person

Documentation Location

Notes

Retirement Benefits

Name

Account Number

Contact Person

Documentation Location

Notes

Retirement Benefits #2

Name

Account Number

Contact Person

Documentation Location

Notes

Social Security

Name

Account Number

Contact Person

Documentation Location

Notes

Other: *Veteran's Benefits, Etc.*

Name

Account Number

Contact Person

Documentation Location

Notes

Other

Name

Account Number

Contact Person

Documentation Location

Notes

Other

Name

Account Number

Contact Person

Documentation Location

Notes

Other - Money Owed to Me

Name

Account Number

Contact Person

Documentation Location

Notes

Name

Account Number

Contact Person

Documentation Location

Notes

Name

Account Number

Contact Person

Documentation Location

Notes

Personal Items, Jewelry, and Heirlooms

Item

Location

Notes

Item

Location

Notes

Item

Location

Notes

Item

Location

Notes

Personal Items, Jewelry, and Heirlooms

Item

Location

Notes

Item

Location

Notes

Item

Location

Notes

Item

Location

Notes

Personal Items, Jewelry, and Heirlooms

Item

Location

Notes

Item

Location

Notes

Item

Location

Notes

Item

Location

Notes

Personal Items, Jewelry, and Heirlooms

Item

Location

Notes

Item

Location

Notes

Item

Location

Notes

Item

Location

Notes

Personal Items, Jewelry, and Heirlooms

Item

Location

Notes

Item

Location

Notes

Item

Location

Notes

Item

Location

Notes

Personal Items, Jewelry, and Heirlooms

Item

Location

Notes

Item

Location

Notes

Item

Location

Notes

Item

Location

Notes

Storage: Company Name

Address

Key Location or Combination Number

Storage: Company Name

Address

Key Location or Combination Number

Notes and Instructions

Business Information

Business Details

Business Name

BusinesType

Address

Landlord Name

Contact Information

Lease Documentation Location

Partner / Co-Owner Name

Contact Information

Partner / Co-Owner Name

Contact Information

Partner / Co-Owner Name

Contact Information

Partner / Co-Owner Name

Contact Information

Keys Location

Notes

Associates, Employees, and Contractors

Name

Contact Information

Name

Contact Information

Name

Contact Information

Name

Contact Information

Name

Contact Information

Name

Contact Information

Name

Contact Information

Name

Contact Information

Notes

Name

Contact Information

Name

Contact Information

Name

Contact Information

Name

Contact Information

Name

Contact Information

Name

Contact Information

Name

Contact Information

Name

Contact Information

Name

Contact Information

Notes

Bank Name

Address

Contact Information

Business Bank Account Number

Business Bank Account Number

Credit Card Number

Username / PIN

Credit Card Number

Username / PIN

Documentation Location

Notes

Bank Name

Address

Contact Information

Business Bank Account Number

Business Bank Account Number

Credit Card Number

Username / PIN

Credit Card Number

Username / PIN

Documentation Location

Notes

Accountant Name

Contact Information

Lawyer

Contact Information

Insurance Agency / Agent

Contact Information

Notes on Income, Royalties, Key Accounts Etc.

Business Website Name

Hosting Provider

Username and Password

Website Developer Name

Contact Information

Documentation Location

Online Income Stream #1

Online Income Stream #2

Partner / Co-Owner Name

Contact Information

Partner / Co-Owner Name

Contact Information

Partner / Co-Owner Name

Contact Information

Business Email Address Name

Username and Password

Business Email Address Name

Username and Password

Business Email Address Name

Username and Password

Notes

Notes: *Instructions for Domain Name Renewal, Hosting, Expenses, Etc.*

Notes: *Instructions for Domain Name Renewal, Monthly Hosting and Expenses, Etc.*

Social Media

Name

Username and Password

Name

Username and Password

Name

Username and Password

Name

Username and Password

Name

Username and Password

Name

Username and Password

Name

Username and Password

Name

Username and Password

Name

Username and Password

Name

Username and Password

Accounts

Name

Username and Password

Name

Username and Password

Name

Username and Password

Name

Username and Password

Name

Username and Password

Name

Username and Password

Name

Username and Password

Name

Username and Password

Name

Username and Password

Name

Username and Password

Accounts

Name

Username and Password

Name

Username and Password

Name

Username and Password

Name

Username and Password

Name

Username and Password

Name

Username and Password

Name

Username and Password

Name

Username and Password

Name

Username and Password

Money I Owe to Others

Person / Company Name

Contact Information

Documentation Location

Notes

Person / Company Name

Contact Information

Documentation Location

Notes

Person / Company Name

Contact Information

Documentation Location

Notes

Person / Company Name

Contact Information

Documentation Location

Notes

Additional Details

Instructions

Banking Information

Bank Name

Account Type and Number

Account Type and Number

Bank Online Web Address

Username and Password

Debit Card Number

Credit Card Number

CV and Password

Online Username and Password

Rewards

Notes

Bank Name

Account Type and Number

Account Type and Number

Bank Online Web Address

Username and Password

Debit Card Number

Credit Card Number

CV and Password

Online Username and Password

Rewards

Notes

Banking Information

Account Type and Number

Account Type and Number

Bank Online Web Address

Username and Password

Debit Card Number

Credit Card Number

CV and Password

Online Username and Password

Rewards

Notes

Safe Deposit Box

Bank Location

Box Number

Key Location

Contents

Safe Deposit Box

Bank Location

Box Number

Key Location

Contents

Other Cards: *Credit, Line of Credit, Department Stores, Etc.*

Name

Account Number

Online Website

Username and Password

Name

Account Number

Online Website

Username and Password

Name

Account Number

Online Website

Username and Password

Name

Account Number

Online Website

Username and Password

Name

Account Number

Online Website

Username and Password

Notes

Other Cards: *Credit, Line of Credit, Department Stores, Etc.*

Name

Account Number

Online Website

Username and Password

Name

Account Number

Online Website

Username and Password

Name

Account Number

Online Website

Username and Password

Name

Account Number

Online Website

Username and Password

Name

Account Number

Online Website

Username and Password

Notes

Other Cards: *Credit, Line of Credit, Department Stores, Etc.*

Name

Account Number

Online Website

Username and Password

Name

Account Number

Online Website

Username and Password

Name

Account Number

Online Website

Username and Password

Name

Account Number

Online Website

Username and Password

Name

Account Number

Online Website

Username and Password

Notes

Mortgage, Line of Credit, Loans

Mortgage Details

Bank / Lender

Contact Information

Account Number

Documentation Location

Mortgage Details

Bank / Lender

Contact Information

Account Number

Documentation Location

Second Mortgage Details

Bank / Lender

Contact Information

Account Number

Documentation Location

Bank / Lender

Contact Information

Account Number

Documentation Location

Notes

Banking Information

Line of Credit

Bank / Lender

Contact Information

Account Number

Documentation Location

Line of Credit

Bank / Lender

Contact Information

Account Number

Documentation Location

Other

Lender

Contact Information

Account Number

Documentation Location

Other

Lender

Contact Information

Account Number

Documentation Location

Notes

Banking Information

Loans: *Cars, Student Loan, Etc.*

Bank / Lender

Contact Information

Account Number

Documentation Location

Bank / Lender

Contact Information

Account Number

Documentation Location

Bank / Lender

Contact Information

Account Number

Documentation Location

Bank / Lender

Contact Information

Account Number

Documentation Location

Bank / Lender

Contact Information

Account Number

Documentation Location

Notes

Important Documents Location

Will Location

____

____

Notes _______________________________

Health Care Power of Attorney Documentation Location

____

____

Notes _______________________________

Passport Location

____

____

Notes _______________________________

Birth Certificate Location

____

____

Notes _______________________________

____

Social Security Number Location

Notes

Drivers Licence Location

Notes

Marriage Certificate

Notes

Tax Documents Location

Notes

Divorce Papers Location

Notes

Life Insurance Location

Notes

Health Insurance Location - Medical

Notes

Health Insurance Location – Dental

Notes

Health Insurance Location - Vision

Notes

Health Insurance Location – Funeral / Other

Notes

Vehicle Insurance Location

Notes

Vehicle Insurance Location #2

Notes

Vehicle Insurance Location #3

Notes

Home Owner Insurance Location

Notes

Rental Home Insurance Location

Notes

Children's Insurance Location

Notes

Additional Family / Dependents Insurance Location

Notes

Pet Insurance Location

Notes

Pet Insurance

Notes

Storage Insurance

Notes

Other

Notes

Other

Notes

Other

Notes

Other

Notes

Other

Notes

Insurance Information

Health Insurance

Company Name

Agents Name

Contact Information

HSA (Health Savings Account) Information

Health Insurance - Dental

Company Name

Agents Name

Contact Information

Health Insurance – Vision

Company Name

Agents Name

Contact Information

Health Insurance – Medical / Other

Company Name

Agents Name

Contact Information

Life Insurance

Company Name

Agents Name

Contact Information

Funeral Insurance

Company Name

Agents Name

Contact Information

Vehicle Insurance

Company Name

Agents Name

Contact Information

Vehicle Insurance

Company Name

Agents Name

Contact Information

Vehicle Insurance

Company Name

Agents Name

Contact Information

Home Owners Insurance

Company Name

Agents Name

Contact Information

Rental Home Insurance

Company Name

Agents Name

Contact Information

Children's Insurance

Company Name

Agents Name

Contact Information

Children's Insurance

Company Name

Agents Name

Contact Information

Children's Insurance

Company Name

Agents Name

Contact Information

Other Dependents Insurance

Company Name

Agents Name

Contact Information

Other Dependents Insurance

Company Name

Agents Name

Contact Information

Pet Insurance

Company Name

Agents Name

Contact Information

Pet Insurance

Company Name

Agents Name

Contact Information

Storage Insurance

Company Name

Agents Name

Contact Information

Other Insurance

Company Name

Agents Name

Contact Information

Other Insurance

Company Name

Agents Name

Contact Information

Other Insurance

Company Name

Agents Name

Contact Information

Other Insurance

Company Name

Agents Name

Contact Information

Other Insurance

Company Name

Agents Name

Contact Information

Medical Information

Health Care Power of Attorney

Name

Contact Information

Do Not Resuscitate Instructions Document Location

Organ Donor Instructions Document Location

Blood Type

Primary Care Physician

Name

Contact Information

Address

Medical Conditions

Medications

Allergies, Food Sensitivity, and Reactions

If Incapacitated Please Follow Below Requests (Further Details in DNR Document)

Preferred Hospital

Name

Contact Information

Address

Pharmacy

Name

Contact Information

Address

Caregiver Company / Person

Name

Contact Information

Address

Caregiver Company / Person

Name

Contact Information

Address

Dependents Instructions for Care

My Dependents

Name

Relationship

Contact Information

Personal Documentation Location

Health Conditions Documentation Location

Guardianship Instructions Documentation Location

Guardian Name

Contact Information

Primary Care Physician

Contact Information

Notes

Name

Relationship

Contact Information

Personal Documentation Location

Health Conditions Documentation Location_

Guardianship Instructions Documentation Location

Guardian Name

Contact Information

Primary Care Physician

Contact Information

Notes

My Dependents

Name

Relationship

Contact Information

Personal Documentation Location

Health Conditions Documentation Location_

Guardianship Instructions Documentation Location

Guardian Name

Contact Information

Primary Care Physician

Contact Information

Notes

My Dependents

Name

Relationship

Contact Information

Personal Documentation Location

Health Conditions Documentation Location_

Guardianship Instructions Documentation Location

Guardian Name

Contact Information

Primary Care Physician

Contact Information

Notes

Name

Relationship

Contact Information

Personal Documentation Location

Health Conditions Documentation Location_

Guardianship Instructions Documentation Location

Guardian Name

Contact Information

Primary Care Physician

Contact Information

Notes

My Dependents

Name

Relationship

Contact Information

Personal Documentation Location

Health Conditions Documentation Location_

Guardianship Instructions Documentation Location

Guardian Name

Contact Information

Primary Care Physician

Contact Information

Notes

Name / Type of Pet

Name of Veterinarian

Contact Information

Address

License, Insurance, and Documentation Location

Health Conditions

Medications

Guardianship Instructions Documentation Location

Guardian Name

Contact Information

General Instructions of Care – Food, Habits, Exercise, Sleep, and Other Needs

Name / Type of Pet ____

Name of Veterinarian ____

Contact Information ____

Address ____

____

License, Insurance, and Documentation Location __________________________

____

Health Conditions ____

____

____

Medications ____

____

____

Guardianship Instructions Documentation Location _______________________

____

Guardian Name ____

Contact Information ____

General Instructions of Care – Food, Habits, Exercise, Sleep, and Other Needs

____

____

____

____

____

My Dependents – Pets

Name / Type of Pet

Name of Veterinarian

Contact Information

Address

License, Insurance, and Documentation Location

Health Conditions

Medications

Guardianship Instructions Documentation Location

Guardian Name

Contact Information

General Instructions of Care – Food, Habits, Exercise, Sleep, and Other Needs

My Dependents — Notes

Follow Up: Cancel, Close, Pay, Change of Name, Etc.

Example: Hydro, Electric, Phone, Cable, Internet, Storage, Credit Cards, Autopay, Banking...

Company / Contact Information

Account Number

Username and Password

Notes

Company / Contact Information

Account Number

Username and Password

Notes

Company / Contact Information

Account Number

Username and Password

Notes

Company / Contact Information

Account Number

Username and Password

Notes

Company / Contact Information

Account Number

Username and Password

Notes

Company / Contact Information

Account Number

Username and Password

Notes

Company / Contact Information

Account Number

Username and Password

Notes

Company / Contact Information

Account Number

Username and Password

Notes

Company / Contact Information

Account Number

Username and Password

Notes

Company / Contact Information

Account Number

Username and Password

Notes

Company / Contact Information

Account Number

Username and Password

Notes

Company / Contact Information

Account Number

Username and Password

Notes

Company / Contact Information

Account Number

Username and Password

Notes

Company / Contact Information

Account Number

Username and Password

Notes

Company / Contact Information

Account Number

Username and Password

Notes

Company / Contact Information

Account Number

Username and Password

Notes

Company / Contact Information

Account Number

Username and Password

Notes

Company / Contact Information

Account Number

Username and Password

Notes

Company / Contact Information

Account Number

Username and Password

Notes

Company / Contact Information

Account Number

Username and Password

Notes

Company / Contact Information

Account Number

Username and Password

Notes

Company / Contact Information

Account Number

Username and Password

Notes

Company / Contact Information

Account Number

Username and Password

Notes

Company / Contact Information

Account Number

Username and Password

Notes

Example: Email, Website, Hosting, Social Media, Banking, Amazon and eBay Memberships

Company / Website

Account Number

Username and Password

Notes

Company / Website

Account Number

Username and Password

Notes

Company / Website

Account Number

Username and Password

Notes

Company / Website

Account Number

Username and Password

Notes

Company / Website

Account Number

Username and Password

Notes

Company / Website

Account Number

Username and Password

Notes

Company / Website

Account Number

Username and Password

Notes

Company / Website

Account Number

Username and Password

Notes

Company / Website

Account Number

Username and Password

Notes

Company / Website

Account Number

Username and Password

Notes

Company / Website

Account Number

Username and Password

Notes

Company / Website

Account Number

Username and Password

Notes

Company / Website

Account Number

Username and Password

Notes

Company / Website

Account Number

Username and Password

Notes

Company / Website

Account Number

Username and Password

Notes

Company / Website

Account Number

Username and Password

Notes

Company / Website

Account Number

Username and Password

Notes

Company / Website

Account Number

Username and Password

Notes

Company / Website

Account Number

Username and Password

Notes

Company / Website

Account Number

Username and Password

Notes

Final Wishes and Instructions

Final Wishes and Instructions

Final Wishes and Instructions

Final Wishes and Instructions

A Personal Message for My Loved Ones

A Personal Message for:

A Personal Message for:

A Personal Message for:

A Personal Message for:

A Personal Message for:

A Personal Message for:

A Personal Message for:

A Personal Message for:

A Personal Message for:

Notes

Notes

Notes

Notes

My Final Farewell

Signature

Name and Date

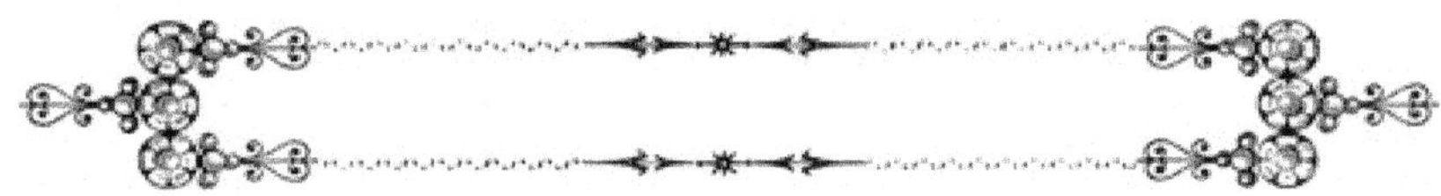